Mentoring:
Developing Successful
New Teachers

Edited by

Theresa M. Bey
and
C. Thomas Holmes

Association of Teacher Educators
Reston, Virginia

Association of Teacher Educators
1900 Association Drive, Suite ATE
Reston, VA 22091

International Standard Book Number: 0-9624818-1-5

Cover design by Virginia Calder, CET, The University of Georgia
Text design and editing by Office of Communication and Publication, G-4 Aderhold Hall, The University of Georgia, Athens, GA 30602. Additional copies may be ordered from the OCP, G-4 Aderhold Hall, The University of Georgia, Athens, GA 30602, (404) 542-0913.

Contents

Acknowledgments

The editors of this publication wish to thank members of the ATE Communications Committee:

John H. McDonnell,
Elaine M. McNiece, and
John Mulhern

for their assistance in reviewing and making suggestions on the manuscript. Also our appreciation is extended to Billy G. Dixon who had the foresight to create the ATE Commission on the Role and Preparation of Mentor Teachers.

The ATE Commission on the Role and Preparation of Mentor Teachers includes the following members.

Theresa Bey, chair	The University of Georgia
Delores Wolfe Eicher	Lynchburg College
Billie Enz	Arizona State
Yvonne Gold	California State at Long Beach
Faye Head	Wake County Public Schools, NC
Leslie Huling-Austin	Southwest Texas State
Richard Kay	Brigham Young University
Steve Marks	Oklahoma State University
Judith C. Neal	California State at Fresno
Sandra Odell	University of New Mexico
Carrie Sedinger	Broward County Schools, FL
Nick Stupiansky	State University of NY/Plattsburg
Tim Young	Central Washington University

Preface

Carl D. Glickman
The University of Georgia

The monograph *Mentoring: Developing Successful New Teachers* appears during a time of an intersection between two school improvement reforms. For twenty years, a legislative reform movement based on "best practice"; regulating, centralizing, and controlling the work of educators has been in vogue. More recently, an empowerment reform movement based on problem solving, decentralizing, and professional decision making has gained momentum. How these competing notions are played out will say much about the status of teaching in the future.

Unless educators have collective choice and responsibility for decisions about their work, *i.e.*, improving teaching and learning, we will continue to lose not only the bright and talented people who we wish to keep, but we will doom our schools to unthinking, lockstep mediocrity. Clearly, the uncaring ways of inducting new persons into teaching will have to go. Our induction process has been an insult to the idea of professionalism. In the past, inverse beginner responsibility has been the most common induction process. Neophyte teachers were "welcomed" to teaching with the least physically desirable classrooms, with less supplies, materials, and furniture; and with the most difficult and challenging students. In most professions, the challenge of the job increases over time as one acquires experience and expertise. In teaching, we've had it reversed. Typically, the most challenging situation a teacher experienced was in his or her first year.

We, as a body of educators, teachers, administrators, state department officials, and university professors, have acknowledged that such a wrong must be made right. The strong case for graduated assimilation of responsibilities has been accepted. Now the challenge is to create professional, personal, and technical support for our beginners. Mentoring is one of the most critical elements for providing such support.

Mentoring, as the authors in this monograph point out, is more than a buddy relationship of social support. Rather, it is a relationship of experienced teachers working with new teachers to inquire about and strengthen instructional competence. In its fullest sense, it is a process that says to people coming into teaching that observing, meeting, discussing, and making informed decisions about teaching and learning is professional work. The immediate end is to help new teachers successfully complete their first years. However, the more important end is to let neophytes know that collegial discussions and planning about the betterment of education for students is an ongoing process of becoming a teacher. The content of this book will assist concerned educators in making decisions about how to achieve the immediate and long term goals of teacher education.

Introduction

Theresa M. Bey
The University of Georgia

A long with the growth of support programs for preservice and inservice teachers has come the practice of mentoring. It's a professional practice that is emerging as a way for experienced teachers, and supervising teachers to offer assistance to new teachers. In fact, their efforts in working with new teachers are causing educators to raise several critical questions. What is the definition of mentoring? What is the role of a mentor? How are mentors to be selected? What are the characteristics of an effective mentor? Do mentors need training? How is the mentor's performance assessed? The need to address these varied questions, as well as contribute significant information to the topic of mentoring is the purpose of this monograph.

Since mentoring is adding a new dimension to teacher support programs, the ATE Commission on the role and Preparation of Mentor Teachers planned for this publication to be a series of articles around the theme of mentoring. So, each chapter is separate and discusses different topics from the perspective and view of an individual author. Even though the chapters are not unified in response to questions and concerns, they are convergent in emphasizing and encouraging the collegial collaboration among teachers.

Given the individualistic nature of each author's chapter, the monograph does not present a definite set of definitions, practices, procedures, conclusions, or recommendations. Instead, it is designed to add to the literature and-expand upon mentoring with the thought that inexperienced teachers stand a better chance of improving their teaching effectiveness with the guidance of a mentor. To be more specific, the first chapter by Sandra Odell, establishes a conceptual basis for offering support to new teachers. Richard Kay's chapter on the principles of mentoring is a support set of guidelines for the mentor's role and responsibility as part of a mentoring relationship. Then, Leslie Huling-Austin's chapter identifies and describes mentoring styles among teachers who work with beginning teachers. Next, Theresa Bey outlines field of study to consider for a knowledge base when preparing mentors. Lastly, C. Thomas Holmes brings closure to the publication by highlighting and synthesizing key aspects of each chapter.

In closing, this monograph is intended for the purpose of provoking further discussion, critical questions, and thoughts about mentoring; as well as giving direction to a goal for educators to share their expertise with others in the effort to strengthen the professional growth of teachers.

Support for New Teachers

Sandra J. Odell
University of New Mexico

Editors' Introduction: As an advocate of support programs for new teachers, the author emphasizes elements that pertain to mentoring within the school environment. More specifically, the elements focus on the roles and characteristics of mentor teachers, applying the mentoring concepts to new teachers, identification of mentors, and the mentor teacher—new teacher relationship.

The past several years have given rise to programs of support for new teachers in literally every state across the country (Neuweiler, 1987). The primary strategy of these programs is to offer structured assistance to beginning teachers to ease their transition from university student to competent instructional leader in the classroom. This strategy assumes that the initial teaching competencies of new teachers are limited and that given structured support, usually by veteran teachers, new teachers will increase their instructional sophistication.

That there has been less than unanimity to date regarding the veteran-teachers' roles in supporting new teachers is reflected in the wide variety of titles that have been assigned to them. These titles have ranged from buddy, through helping teacher or support teacher, to master or advisor. Zimpher and Rieger (1988) have commented on the range of veteran teacher roles that these titles imply. Indeed, a continuum is suggested for the new teacher—veteran teacher relationship with one end of the continuum anchored by a personally-introspective relationship and the other end anchored by an objectively-analytic relationship.

The most widely used title for veteran teachers in support programs has been mentor teacher, probably because this term tends to conjure up the image of a mentor guiding the new teacher along the journey of professional development. In reality, however, the term mentor teacher has been used to describe new teacher—veteran teacher relationships that encompass the entire introspective-analytic continuum of these relationships. Nevertheless, the term mentor teacher will be adopted herein with the caveat that an assigned title only specifies an intended function. It does not guarantee that the intended function will be fully realized.

Substantial attention has also been given to establishing the goals of support programs for new teachers (Odell, 1989) and to empirically analyzing the needs of new teachers receiving structured assistance from veteran teachers (e.g., Odell, 1986b, 1987; Odell, Loughlin, & Ferraro, 1987). In addition to assigning mentor teachers to work with new teachers and specifying goals and support content, it is also necessary to have an effective strategy for delivering that support to new teachers. To date relatively little attention has been given to the conceptual bases that underlie the delivery of such support.

It is the objective of this chapter to identify how the concept of mentoring, as it has been developed outside of the public school setting, provides an important basis from which to develop support strategies for assisting new teachers (cf., Anderson & Shannon, 1988). Effective mentoring relationships will be defined and suggestions for utilizing mentoring strategies for working with beginning teachers will be discussed. In addition, ways of identifying mentor teachers, forming and fostering mentoring relationships, and achieving "significance" in the mentoring relationship will be addressed.

Concept of Mentoring

The origin of the term mentor is found in Homer's epic poem, *The Odyssey*, wherein Odysseus gave the responsibility to his loyal friend, Mentor, of nurturing his son, Telemachus. Odysseus ventured off to fight the Trojan War while Mentor educated and guided his son. "This education was not confined to the martial arts but was to include every facet of his life — physical, intellectual, spiritual, social, and administrative development" (Clawson, 1980, p. 144). Anderson and Shannon (1988) conclude from *The Odyssey* that modeling a standard and style of behavior is a central quality of mentoring and that mentoring is an intentional, nurturing, insightful, supportive, protective process.

Mentoring Relationships and Definitions

The idea of a newcomer entering a career under the guidance and direction of a wise, experienced mentor has been viewed as important in a number of contexts outside of public education. For example, businessmen who had mentors apparently earned more money at a younger age, were more satisfied with their work and career advancement, and were better educated than those without mentors (Bolton, 1980; Roche, 1979).

Bova and Phillips (1983) found that proteges in university and business settings learned risk taking behaviors, communication skills, political skills, and specific professional skills from their mentors. They conclude that mentoring relationships are critical for developing professionals and endorse Levinson's (1978) broad assertion that mentoring is the essence of adult development.

Considering the apparent importance of the mentoring relationship to career and adult development, one might expect that consensual agreement on the defined role of the mentor has been achieved. That such is not the case can be readily gleaned from Table 1, which presents a sampling of suggested mentor roles that appear in the literature [cf., Galvez-Hjornevik (1986) for a comprehensive review of mentor definitions; Huling-Austin (1990) for a delineation of mentor styles; and Kay (1990) for a discussion of mentoring principles]. Obviously, suggested mentor roles have varied in terms of the number of dimensions they encompass and in the heterogeneity of those dimensions. The variation in mentor roles range from protecting and opening doors, to guiding, teaching, and coaching, to consulting, advising, and counseling. Apparently, it is within the mentor role either to accomplish something for the protege, or to teach the protege how to do something, or to advise the protege about what to do.

Not included in Table 1 are some of the more abstract, almost spiritual characteristics sometimes ascribed to the mentor's role (e.g., Gehrke, 1988; Parkay, 1988). In these instances, the mentor-protege relationship is thought to transcend the giving of support to the giving of self on the part of the mentor.

Table 1

A Sampler of Mentor Roles Drawn from the Literature

Mentor Roles	Reference
Trusted guide	Homer's *Odyssey*
Teacher, Sponsor, Host, Counselor, Supporter, Guru, Advisor	Levinson, 1978
Teacher coach, Trainer, Positive role model, Developer of talent, Opener of doors, Protector, Sponsor, Successful leader	Schein, 1978
Traditional mentor, Supportive boss, Organizational sponsor, Professional mentor, Patron, Invisible godparent	Phillips-Jones, 1982
Guide, Supporter, Challenger	Daloz, 1983
Teacher, Counselor, Guide, Supporter, Protector, Promoter, Sponsor	Zey, 1984
Confidant (in addition to Schein's 1978 roles)	Gehrke & Kay, 1984
Master teacher, Teacher adviser, Teacher specialist, Teacher researcher-linker, Consultant	Bird, 1985
Colleague teacher, Helping teacher, Peer teacher, Support teacher	Borko, 1986
Teacher, Sponsor, Encourager, Counselor, Befriender	Anderson & Shannon, 1988

Typically, such a relationship is viewed as forming slowly over time, being complex and emotionally intense, and being of incalculable value (Gehrke, 1988; Gehrke and Kay, 1984).

The term that has been used by Hardcastle (1988) to differentiate this more abstract, interpersonal, life-changing mentoring relationship from other more limited mentoring relationships is "significant mentor." Clawson (1980) offers the concepts of comprehensiveness and mutuality as two means of determining the significance of mentoring relationships. Comprehensiveness refers to the number and variety of dimensions encompassed by the mentoring relationship. A truly comprehensive mentoring relationship incorporates interactions among intellectual development, spiritual growth, personal life, and work. A limited mentoring relationship, in the extreme, is restricted to only one of these dimensions. Mutuality refers to the extent to which the mentoring relationship is voluntarily entered into and warmly regarded by both the protege and mentor.

In a study by Hardcastle (1988), it was determined that while individuals do deliberately search for someone to guide them, mentors and proteges more often happen upon one another in unplanned ways. Kay (1990) identifies important environmental considerations like unselfishness and cooperation that make this occurrence of proteges finding mentors more likely. Using interviews of primarily university protege-mentor relationships, Hardcastle (1988) determined that proteges were attracted to mentors who had integrity and who were wise, caring, and committed to their professions. In addition, high expectations, an ability to act as a catalyst, and a sense of humor were viewed as important mentor characteristics. Proteges also said that desired mentors were able to point out particular strengths of the proteges, to motivate the proteges to grow professionally, and to show them "new ways to be."

Similarly, based on his personal university experience with a mentor, Parkay (1988) described what he felt were the essential conditions of a significant mentoring relationship. These conditions included recognizing the mentor as a seminal contributor to the profession, sharing a similar style of thinking between the mentor and protege, modeling by the mentor of a commitment to a professional way of life, and allowing the protege to determine the direction and mode of learning.

Mentoring New Teachers

The applicability of the concept of mentoring to the design and implementation of support programs for new teachers has been recognized by Anderson and Shannon (1988). They first endorsed five of the mentoring roles found in the general mentoring literature as being basic mentoring functions in a beginning teacher context (teacher, sponsor, encourager, counselor, befriender). They argue effectively that mentoring activities in a public school setting should derive conceptually as expressions of these basic mentoring functions. Agreeing with the general mentoring concept described in the previous section, Anderson and Shannon (1988) further argue that the new teacher — mentor teacher relationship should be significant, and that mentor teachers should have the dispositions of a desired mentor.

While it is the objective of this chapter to reinforce the proposition that the concept of mentoring provides a useful theoretical framework for the development of support programs, a caution seems in order at this point. In deriving practices from mentoring concepts, we must be careful to use our extant knowledge of the stages of teacher development (*e.g.*, Fuller, 1969; Katz, 1972), new teacher needs (*e.g.*, Veenman, 1984; Odell, 1986b), effective inservice teacher education (*e.g.*, Howey, 1985), and analysis of teaching (*e.g.*, Zeichner, 1983) as context. Simply superimposing the mentoring concept isomorphically onto the teacher support situation, and then specifying practices by analogy to mentoring, provides no guarantee that a successful support program for new teachers will be achieved.

As a practical matter, consider that the direct transposition of significant mentoring characteristics to the new teacher — mentor teacher relationship is difficult to achieve in the school setting. Critical components of significant mentoring relationships, namely comprehensiveness and mutuality (Clawson, 1980), are unlikely to be fully realized even in demonstrably successful teacher support programs.

For example, rather than comprehensively dealing with all aspects of intellectual, personal, and spiritual growth, a mentor teacher in a school context is most likely to limit the focus to the professional growth of the new teacher. Similarly, the goal of mutuality cannot always be achieved inasmuch as practical considerations may require that mentor teachers be assigned to new teachers rather than allowing mentors and new teachers to choose one another freely (Odell, 1986a). Moreover, the sometimes imposed requirement that mentor teachers make future employment assessments of new teachers can limit the development of significant mentoring relationships (Feiman-Nemser, Odell, & Lawrence, 1988), as can the short duration of time, usually one year, that most support or mentor programs are in effect (Brooks, 1987).

The offered cautions and practical limitations not withstanding, much of what works in supporting new teachers can trace its heritage to the concept of mentoring. These applications of mentoring go more to the strategies of developing and delivering support than they do to the goals and content of support. It is to these applications that we turn next.

Applying The Mentoring Concept

This section will apply the mentoring concept to the matter of identifying mentor teachers, forming new teacher—mentor teacher relationships, fostering these relationships, and achieving significance in teacher mentoring relationships. Much of what follows draws heavily from a previous description of the factors involved in developing support programs for beginning teachers (Odell, 1989).

Identifying Mentor Teachers

It is obviously desirable for all mentor teachers to be wise, caring, humorous, nurturing, committed to their professions (Hardcastle, 1988; Kay, 1990), and to share the dispositions of openness, leadership and concern (Anderson & Shannon, 1988). Within the boundaries of a support program for new teachers, however, certain other mentor characteristics should be sought when identifying and selecting mentor teachers.

Foremost among these is the recognition that the mentor teacher serves specifically as a role model for the classroom teacher, and may be involved in demonstration teaching, teacher coaching, effective teacher training, or other learner strategies with the new teacher. It follows that a mentor teacher must be an excellent classroom teacher. However, an excellent classroom teacher of children and adolescents is not automatically an excellent mentor teacher. After all, mentor teachers are mentoring other adults. Accordingly, the mentor teacher needs to be an effective teacher of adult learners as well as of young learners.

A mentor teacher needs to possess wisdom in order to be found desirable as a mentor by new teachers. The specific wisdom needed by a mentor teacher includes knowledge of the stages of teacher development, the needs of beginning teachers, effective instructional strategies, and the cognitive bases of problem solving and critical thinking.

Not only will the mentor teacher need to demonstrate competency and wisdom in the practice and theory of teaching, but the mentor teacher also needs to transmit these to the new teacher by guiding, advising, and supporting the practice of the new teacher. Mentor teachers who possess skill in reflective listening and effective questioning will master the mentor teacher role with the greatest efficacy and sensitivity. Mentor teachers should be facile at conflict resolution, not only to minimize communication barriers to the new teacher but also to protect, promote, and sponsor the new teacher in interactions with other teachers, school administrators, and parents.

While the mentor teacher is unlikely to significantly impact upon the personal domain of the new teacher, or to truly befriend or enter into an intense emotional relationship with the new teacher, the mentor teacher should strive to impact the new teacher as comprehensively and multidimensionally as possible within the school setting. Clearly, the mentor needs to deal with the survival anxieties, self concept issues, and reality shock surrounding teaching that sometimes engulf the new teacher (Veenman, 1984). Mentor teachers can most readily provide personal support related to the teaching context if they are versed in problem-solving skills and have the personal attributes of being empathic, gregarious, caring, and adaptable.

The provision of emotional support can be a seductive activity. It is important for the mentor teacher to have the capacity of setting limits on the domains of personal and spiritual growth that will be addressed within the new teacher — mentor teacher relationship. This will serve both to keep the interactions with the new teacher within the assumed competencies of the mentor teacher and to retain the primary focus of the interactions on the professional development of the new teacher.

Forming The Mentoring Relationship

As has been discussed above, significant mentor relationships sometimes form as a result of happenstance and often form through the mutual choice of the mentor and protege, particularly where they have a high regard for one another. For the most part, however, protege — mentor relationships are created by assignment in schools. This lack of mutuality results most often from unavoidable practical program considerations (*e.g.*, who in the school is interested and available to be a mentor, and who was hired this year as a new teacher in the school). Assigning mentors to new teachers increases the likelihood that a particular protege — mentor teacher duo will not enter into an effective mentoring relationship. The best approach to forming the mentoring relationship obviously remains to offer new and veteran teachers some choice in selecting with whom they will work. Where assignment is necessary, it is desirable to retain enough flexibility of assignment to permit reassignment if a particular new teacher — mentor teacher bond does not form.

Inasmuch as mentor teachers serve as teacher role models, it is helpful to assign mentor teachers by matching the grade level and content areas of the mentor and new teacher. If nothing else, this match imbues the mentor teacher with more face validity for the new teacher.

Parkay (1988) has suggested that mentoring relationships form best when a similar style of thinking is shared between the mentor and protege. Within the school environment, this translates most directly into assigning mentor teachers by matching their teaching style and ideology to that of the new teacher. It seems obvious on the surface that a new teacher who is enthusiastic about teaching with an informal, open, and innovative style will be better guided, sponsored, supported, and even protected by a like-minded mentor than by a mentor who is committed professionally and personally to another teaching approach. This is not to say that a mentor teacher should not challenge the new teacher to promote intellectual and professional growth. But a significant mentor is rarely dogmatic or proscriptive, and always strives to establish a relationship in which a sensitivity and openness to the style and ideology of the new teacher is demonstrated. Such a constructive, productive relationship forms most rapidly when common views are held from the outset of the mentoring relationship.

Demographically, it appears that the sex of the mentor and new teacher should be the same, and that new teachers should be assigned mentors who are older. Apparently, there are fewer conflicts not relevant to mentoring among similar sex teachers (Hunt & Michael, 1983; Kram, 1983), and a new teacher can be predicted to bond more readily to a mentor who is 10 to 15 years older (*e.g.,* Levinson, 1978).

A final logistical consideration pointed out by Odell (1989) in forming mentoring relationships is that new teachers should have ready physical access to their mentors. If the mentor appears too infrequently in the classroom of the new teacher, or the new teacher must traverse the school grounds in order to be supported by the mentor, the likelihood is diminished that immediate and continuous support over time will occur.

Fostering the Mentor Relationship

Once the mentoring relationship is formed, it can be nurtured to develop into a mature relationship characterized by mutual trust. Odell (1989) has suggested that a first step in fostering a mentoring relationship is for the mentor and new teacher to get to know one another. She suggests that this can best be accomplished through informal one-on-one meetings outside of the teaching day and, perhaps, somewhere off the school grounds where a supportive level of comfort can be more readily achieved by both mentor and new teacher.

The mentoring relationship is further fostered to the extent that the new teacher understands that the mentor's role is to guide and support the new teacher's study of the process of teaching. This understanding requires that the mentor appreciates and respects the viewpoints of the new teacher, recognizes the strengths of the new teacher, and guides the new teacher to self identify individual needs as a teacher. This guiding can be effectively accomplished by adapting peer-coaching strategies so that the new teacher is coached by the mentor to analyze teaching reflectively (Joyce & Showers, 1982).

A third positive influence is the development of respect by the new teacher for the competency, knowledge, and wisdom of the mentor. This respect is not inherent in the title "mentor," but is earned by the mentor. The new teacher develops this respect over time as the mentor repeatedly provides guidance and feedback that improves the new teacher's instructional competency, support to the teaching function, pertinent advice, and emotional support that helps the new teacher cope better. The mentor teacher should demonstrate competency in these areas. One effective and productive means of doing so is through the early and extensive use of demonstration teaching.

Ultimately what is sought in the mentoring relationship is a mutual trust and belief in one another. This is more easily achieved in an assistance-based program (Feiman-Nemser, Odell, & Lawrence, 1988). The distinction here is that in an assistance-based than in an assessment-based mentoring process, evaluations of new-teacher performance by mentor teachers are done for the sole purpose of facilitating the teachers' professional development. In an assessment-based process, evaluation of new teachers by mentor teachers are used to determine whether new teachers have mastered teaching competencies sufficiently well to be certified and/or retained on the instructional staff.

New teachers report that the benefits of a mentor relationship depend upon their feeling safe in the relationship. New teachers also consider a feeling of trust as necessary so that candid self analysis of their teaching needs, concerns, and deficiencies will not occasion adverse employment outcomes (Fox & Singletary, 1986; Huffman & Leak, 1986).

It is for these and other related reasons that it has been argued (Brooks, 1987) that the assistance and evaluative functions should be assigned to different personnel in a school setting. Clearly, from the concept of mentoring, only the assistance function is consonant with a significant mentoring relationship. Stated quite succinctly, "mentors" who engage in evaluations for future employment decisions are not mentoring (*e.g.,* Klopf & Harrison, 1983).

Achieving Significance in the Mentoring Relationship

In the literature, mentors are found to be significant when they impact the protege comprehensively and multidimensionally, that is across personal and professional life dimensions (*e.g.,* Hardcastle, 1988). Given the focus on professional development that is demanded of mentors, a mentor teacher will only rarely achieve significance in this comprehensive sense. There is, however, another sense in which the new teacher—mentor teacher relationship can achieve significance. This occurs when the mentoring relationships provides the new teacher with independence from the mentor teacher in studying the teaching process.

Mentors are usually considered to exert their influence over the long term. However, the usual new teacher—mentor teacher relationship typically lasts for only the duration of the first school year. It seems generally unlikely, from a fiscal perspective, that the mentoring relationship will be routinely extended to the second and third school years in the future, though a conceptually strong argument could be made for such an extension.

What this suggests is that mentors should work to prepare new teachers to mentor themselves; to become, so to speak, automentors. Achieving significance in this sense can be an aspiration if the mentor teacher adopts a mentoring style that is neither too emotionally supportive nor too professionally directive but is interactive. That is, the mentor teacher can combine support given with guiding the new teacher to be a self-analytic, reflective, independent learner about the teaching process. Again, the goal of the mentor teacher is to imbue the new teacher with the conviction that only in being a life-long student of the teaching process can one develop fully as a classroom teacher. It seems probable, when all is said and done, that the process of learning to automentor is the same process as developing as a mentor teacher for others who are to be inducted into the teaching profession.

References

Anderson, E.M., & Shannon, S.L. (1988). Toward a conceptualization of mentoring. *Journal of Teacher Education*, **39**(1), 38-42.

Bird, T. (1985). *From teacher to leader: Training and support for mentor teachers, master teachers, and teacher advisors.* Unpublished manuscript, The Far West Regional Laboratory, San Francisco.

Borko, H. (1986). Clinical teacher education: The induction years. In J.V. Hoffman & S.A. Edwards (Eds.), *Reality and reform in clinical teacher education* (pp. 45-63). New York: Random House.

Bolton, E. (1980). A conceptual analysis of the mentor relationship in the career development of women. *Adult Education*, **30**(4), 195-297.

Bova, B.M., & Phillips, R. (1983). Mentoring revisited: An investigation of the learning component. *Mountain Plains Adult Education Association*, **11**(2), 21-32.

Brooks, D.M. (Ed.) (1987). *Teacher induction: A new beginning.* Reston, VA: Association of Teacher Educators..

Clawson, J.G. (1980). In C.B. Derr (Ed.)., *Work, family and the career* (pp. 144-165). New York: Praeger.

Daloz, L.A. (1983), Mentors: Teachers who make a difference. *Change*, **15**(6), 24-27.

Feiman-Nemser, S., Odell, S.J., & Lawrence, D. (1988). Induction programs and the professionalization of teachers: Two views. *Colloquay*, **1**(2), 11-19.

Fox, S.M., & Singletary, T.J. (1986). Deductions about supportive induction. *Journal of Teacher Education*, **37**(1), 12-15.

Fuller, F.F. (1969). Concerns of teachers: A development conceptualization. *American Educational Research Journal*, **6**, 207-226.

Futrell, M.H. (1988). Selecting and compensating mentor teachers: A win-win scenario. *Theory Into Practice*, **27**(3), 223-225.

Galvez-Hjornevik, C. (1986). Mentoring among teachers: A review of the literature. *Journal of Teacher Education*, **37**(1), 6-11.

Gehrke, N. (1988). Toward a definition of mentoring. *Journal of Teacher Education*, **39**(1), 190-194.

Gehrke, N., & Kay, R.S. (1984). Socialization of beginning teachers through mentor-protege relationships. *Journal of Teaching Education*, **35**(3), 12-14.

Hardcastle, B. (1988). Spiritual connections: Proteges' reflections on significant mentorships. *Theory Into Practice*, **27**(3), 201-208.

Howey, K. (1985). Six major functions of staff development: An expanded imperative. *Journal of Teacher Education*, **36**(1), 58-64.

Huffman, G., & Leak, S. (1986). Beginning teachers' perceptions of mentors. *Journal of Teacher Education*, **37**(1), 22-25.

Huling-Austin, L. L. (1990). Mentoring is squishy business. In T. M. Bey & C. T. Holmes (Eds.), *Mentoring: Developing Successful New Teachers*. Reston, VA: Association of Teacher Educators.

Hunt, D.M., & Michael, C. (1983). Mentorship: A career training and development tool. *Academy of Management Review*, **8**(3), 475-485.

Joyce, B.R., & Showers, B. (1982). The coaching of teaching. *Educational Leadership*, **40**, 4-10.

Katz, L.G. (1972). Developmental stages of preschool teachers. *Elementary School Journal*, **73**, 50-54.

Kay, R. S. (1990). Mentoring: Definition, principles, and applications. In T. M. Bey & C. T. Holmes (Eds.), *Mentoring: Developing Successful New Teachers*. Reston, VA: Association of Teacher Educators.

Klopf, G., & Harrison, J. (1981, September). Moving up the career ladder: A case for mentors. *Principal*, **61**, 41-43.

Kram, K.E. (1983). Phases of the mentor relationship. *Academy of Management Journal*, **26**(4), 608-625.

Levinson, D. (1978). *The Seasons of a Man's Life*. New York: Knopf.

Neuweiler, H.B. (1987). *Teacher Education Policy in*

the States: Fifty-state Survey of Legislative and Administrative Action. Washington, D.C.: American Association of Colleges for Teacher Education.

Odell, S.J. (1986a). A model university-school system collaboration in teacher induction. *Kappa Delta Pi Record,* **22**(4), 120-121.

Odell, S.J. (1986b). Induction support of new teachers: A functional approach. *Journal of Teacher Education,* **37**(1), 26-29.

Odell, S.J. (1987). Teacher induction: Rationale and issues. In D. Brooks (Ed.), *Teacher Induction: A New Beginning.* Reston, VA: Association of Teacher Educators.

Odell, S.J. (1989). Developing support programs for beginning teachers. In R.A. Edelfelt (Ed.), *Beginning Teacher Assistance Programs.* Reston VA: Association of Teacher Educators.

Odell, S.J., Loughlin, C.E., & Ferraro, D.P. (1987). Functional approach to identification of new teacher needs in an induction context. *Action in Teacher Education,* **8**(4), 51-57.

Parkay, F.W. (1988). Reflections of a protege. *Theory Into Practice,* **27**(3), 195-200.

Phillips-Jones, L. (1982). *Mentors and Proteges.* New York: Arbor House.

Roche, G.R. (1979). Much ado about mentors. *Harvard Business Review,* **57**(1), 14-16, 20, 24-27.

Schein, E. (1978). *Career Dynamics: Matching individual and organizational needs*. Reading, MA: Addison-Wesley.

Veenman, S. (1984). Perceived problems of beginning teachers. *Review of Educational Research*, **54**(2), 143-178.

Zeichner, K. (1983). Alternative paradigms of teacher education. *Journal of Teacher Education*, **34**(3), 3-9.

Zey, M.G. (1984). *The mentor connection*. Homewood, IL: Dow Jones-Irwin.

Zimpher, N.L., & Rieger, S.R. (1988). Mentoring teachers: What are the issues? *Theory Into Practice*, **27**(3), 175-181.

A Definition for Developing Self-Reliance

Richard S. Kay
Brigham Young University-Utah

Editors' Introduction: Self-reliance and accountability are considered to be fundamental aspects of mentoring. They not only reflect the author's definition of mentoring, they also support his discussion of the principles of mentoring within the framework of a Responsibility Model for Mentors.

Mentoring is a current educational practice widely incorporated into beginning teacher assistance programs. In these programs, experienced educators, usually classroom teachers, are assigned as mentors to work with the beginning teachers and provide assistance to help them make effective, non-traumatic transitions into full-time teaching. Current education and business journals are replete with articles on mentoring, each making a contribution at some level to an understanding of the factors underlying the description, establishment and/or maintenance of effective mentor-protege relationships. Included in these sources are several attempts at defining mentoring, none of which are totally satisfactory for guiding systematic investigation and development. This chapter has two purposes: (1) to offer a workable definition of "mentoring" that can be used as a foundation for further investigation and development efforts and (2) to articulate a set of principles or guidelines for mentoring that will encourage and support productive mentoring activities and relationships.

Not Just A Relationship

Human developmental theories indicate the presence of a universal human need and motive toward competence and being able to succeed. White (1959) says that the human potential for thinking and reasoning would be a damnation to the organism were it not for, as he puts it, "...a steady, persistent inclination toward interacting with the environment." He says, "there is a competence motivation...[and that this motivation]...satisfies an intrinsic need to deal with the environment." White refers to this competence in dealing with the environment as "effectance." Bandura (1977) developed a theory of social learning based on what he calls "self-efficacy" or the belief in one's own capability to successfully perform a task. Bandura's social-learning theory and White's theory of motivation incorporate many of the same assumptions and principles; both emphasize the importance of competency and being able to do for one's self. Peck (1974) and Glasser (1965) are among many educators and clinicians who emphasize the need to help people develop patterns of responsible behavior antecedent to emotional well-being and adequate adjustment of the individual within society. Glasser (1965) says that the most important lesson that can be taught in our society is responsibility. Kay (1989) defines responsibility as, "Exercising one's own powers and judgments (self-reliance) with a sense of moral and ethical obligation to self and others (accountability)." The proposed definition of mentoring is based on the assumption that it is in the individual's and society's best interests for everyone to learn responsibility. *Mentoring is a comprehensive effort directed toward helping a protege develop the attitudes and behaviors (skills) of self-reliance and accountability within a defined environment.*

This definition of mentoring can be more clearly understood by examining each of its parts. First, mentoring is a comprehensive effort which brings together sufficient resources to have an intense impact on the development of the protege. This results in the development of attitudes and skills that have broad application within the protege's environment. In Greek mythology, Mentor was given total responsibility for the guidance and education of Telemachus. This responsibility required a major time and energy commitment from Mentor. Because Telemachus was dependent upon the guidance provided by Mentor, Mentor was faced with providing the type of help and assistance that would have maximum application in Telemachus's life. Mentor taught Telemachus to think and do things for himself.

A protege is an individual who is both a recipient of assistance and a participant in a comprehensive effort toward becoming self-reliant and accountable. Clawson (1980) indicates that *mutual participation* is an essential ingredient to any effective mentor-protege relationship. Mentoring is not an activity where the mentor imposes change on an unsuspecting protege. Given the above definition, the success of the mentoring effort requires that the protege actively seeks to become self-reliant.

The attitudes and behaviors of self-reliance are an open set of attitudes and skills that are identified as instrumental to the success of the protege within the context of mentoring. These attitudes and skills for success and self-reliance fall into two possible categories; those that are generic and have application in a wide variety of contexts and those that are more specific to the context in which the mentoring occurs. One mentoring model (Kay, 1989) specifies three attitudes or beliefs and six skills which are generic and tend to influence the willingness and abilities of individuals to act with self-reliance. Self-reliant people tend to have the attitudes that they: (1) are competent and able to successfully do things for themselves, (2) can influence the conditions and circumstances of their own lives through their efforts in applying their abilities, and (3) have personal worth that is unconditional and independent of their actions, possessions, accomplishments and other contingencies. Self-reliant people also have the skills to: (1) identify appropriate standards for making personal comparisons and decisions, (2) observe and collect objective information about their own efforts, progress, and accomplishments, (3) collect valid information from other appropriate sources, (4) make comparisons between the information collected and designated standards to obtain feedback and make decisions, (5) use the feedback they receive to make needed improvements and modifications, and (6) affirm and sustain themselves by relying on personally controlled, intrinsic reinforcements.

Accountability is the realization of obligation to act in accordance with established standards and the willingness to have those actions evaluated accordingly. The most productive type of accountability is where each individual holds him/herself accountable and does not require policing or direction by others to act productively and in a manner beneficial to self and society. This type of accountability is possible when individuals systematically apply the skills of self-reliance as stated (Kay, 1989).

A defined environment is the context within which the protege is being prepared toward self-reliance, success and accountability. The context of mentoring for a beginning teacher may be limited to his/her role as a classroom teacher and the various responsibilities included in that role or the relationship may go beyond teaching to include more personal areas. The context may be defined any way the protege and those providing the mentoring are willing for it to be defined.

A mentor is a person participating in a significant way as part of a comprehensive effort toward helping a protege become self-reliant and accountable. In the present definition, mentoring is treated as a function rather than as a relationship. In doing so many existing relational and organizational limitations imposed on mentoring are displaced. Typically, mentoring is viewed as a superior-subordinate dyad which makes it difficult to implement in teacher induction programs given the constraints and limitations of most educational settings. Under the present definition, one-on-one relationships are not required for mentoring nor are they precluded; they are only one of several possible configurations in which mentoring may occur. It is possible, for example, for several individuals to be part of a simultaneous mentoring effort directed toward one or more proteges. It is also possible, and exciting, to think of total environments where all the dimensions of the context including the personnel, resources, and operating procedures of that environment contribute to a mentoring effort. These mentoring environments can be created within grade level teaching groups, subject matter departments and even entire schools. The definition also allows for one person to mentor many proteges simultaneously by behaving toward those proteges according to mentoring principles and guidelines. The building principal, as an example, can provide comprehensive assistance to an entire faculty by the way he/she works with them and the way in which he/she structures and operates the school and its programs.

In addition to opening new configurations for mentoring, the present definition identifies a focus for the effort that is so often missing in other definitions. Definitions which focus primarily on describing mentoring usually do nothing more than that. Such descriptive definitions tend to equate current practice with the ideal. In reading these articles, one might assume that such behavior descriptions represent the "How" of mentoring and how mentors should treat proteges. What "IS" as described in the literature does not necessarily portray what "SHOULD BE." For example, Levinson (1978) reported that some mentor-protege relationships end with anger or bitterness. Such endings can be avoided if the motives of the mentor and the protege are in harmony and mutually understood. A definition which articulates a purpose can provide useful direction for the creation and encouragement of the ideal. Providing help and assistance focusing on self-reliance automatically eliminates actions and relationships which hinder the development of protege control and responsibility. Self-reliance is contrary to dependence which can be unintentionally encouraged in a misguided mentor-protege relationship. Having provided a definition, the focus now moves to the second purpose of this chapter; to provide selected principles for guiding mentoring efforts and activities.

Some "Shoulds" for Mentoring

The same theories which contributed to the definition of mentoring are the foundation for a set of principles which can be used to guide mentoring efforts. The following six principles for mentoring, derived from many areas of investigation including theories of learning, motivation, human development and organizational behavior, articulate some of the "SHOULDS" on how to help people develop the attitudes and skills of self-reliance and accountability. These principles are part of a Responsibility Model for Mentoring (Kay, 1989).

Principle #1: Self-reliance is facilitated when the protege receives encouragement and unconditional acceptance.

Encouragement comes through knowing what to do, how to do it and having the opportunity to do so. Encouragement also comes through knowing that mistakes and failures are not final or irreversible. Mentoring offers training in requisite skills necessary for success in the defined environment, opportunities to practice those skills in meaningful contexts, and the opportunity to learn from those efforts. An underlying attitude of unconditional acceptance confirms the protege's unchanged acceptability as a person, regardless of the success or failure in the task(s). A mentoring environment must be emotionally safe where the protege can feel free to try new things without fear of non-retrievable losses.

Principle #2: The limits on the comprehensiveness of the mentoring relationship are defined through

mutual consent of the mentor(s) and the protege.

Mentoring cannot be mandated; mentors must be willing to help and the proteges must be willing to receive their help before mentoring can proceed. Mentor offered his help to Telemachus but it was Telemachus who made the decision to accept or reject Mentor's help. Mentoring in beginning teacher induction programs where fellow teachers serve as mentors is often inhibited by reluctance on the part of the mentor and/or the protege to initiate such a relationship. Feared *presumptiveness* on the part of the mentor and reluctance to admit *inadequacy* by the protege are often cited as barriers to be overcome in establishing mentoring relationships. Mentoring, when viewed as a function, can be provided by many and entered into informally to reduce the negative connotations sometimes associated with superior-subordinate relationships. People are usually more willing to offer and to receive help when such behaviors are accepted norms in the situation.

Principle #3: The comprehensiveness of a mentoring effort is a function of the resources and expertise made available to the protege.

Mentoring is a comprehensive effort toward helping the protege develop self-reliance and personal accountability. The literature on mentoring and mentor-protege relationships suggests that a mentor has exclusive responsibility for training the protege. This is an ominous responsibility from which many people, who have a great deal to offer, retreat. The comprehensiveness can be increased by assembling and effectively utilizing a variety of available resources. It is not reasonable to assume that one very competent person can provide as much help and expertise as several equally competent people. The idea of mentoring can be extended by including a variety of people in any effort to assist another, assuming of course that each individual is willing to provide such help. Mentoring may include coordinating the efforts and expertise of others in the helping effort. A mentor teacher may initiate contacts for the beginning teacher with other capable teachers in the same building and in doing so provide the beginning teacher with the opportunity to be in contact with additional expertise.

Principle #4: The comprehensiveness of a mentoring effort is a function of the generalizability within the defined environment of the attitudes, skills and behaviors developed by the protege.

A mentor-protege relationship will be more comprehensive if the protege is helped to develop attitudes, skills and behaviors that have broad application and utility within the defined environment. Any mentor-protege relationship is limited in what it can accomplish given the limits of time and availability of resources. Mentoring efforts should yield maximum returns on any and all resources invested in helping the protege. For instance, it was impossible for Mentor to teach Telemachus all the specifics he would need to know to function effectively in life. In fact, if Mentor had tried he would have failed because part of what Telemachus needed to learn was how to think, reason, and learn for himself. Mentors who take upon themselves the responsibility of providing answers for their proteges inhibit the ability of their proteges to find out for themselves. The saying, "Give a man a fish and you feed him once but teach him how to fish and you feed him for life," is very appropriate when trying to provide comprehensive help toward self-reliance.

Principle #5: Mentors should put the growth of their proteges above their own needs except where both can be served without sacrificing the former.

Some individuals engage in helping efforts out of needs within themselves which run counter to the growth of the person they extend themselves toward. Coopersmith and Feldman (1974) make a very good point that those who offer help need to separate their need to provide help from the other person's need to receive help. Mentoring should never involve doing something for a person that the person can benefit most by doing it for him/herself. Mentoring is helping not substituting for the protege. Efforts toward helping another develop self-reliance should not build dependency.

Principle #6: People who are themselves self-reliant are more willing and able to help others become the same.

Those who engage in mentoring efforts are likely to be more effective if they have developed or are working to develop appropriate attitudes and skills within themselves. The theories cited to support the definition of mentoring (*i.e.*, attribution theory, etc.) also suggest that self-reliant people are more likely than dependent people to:

- Seek new opportunities with a positive attitude, anticipating success.

- Cooperate with others without competition or need to control.

- Be genuine in all their relationships and allow others to do the same.

- Accept the change and obligation of meeting their own needs.

- Make their own decisions and not be unduly influenced by others.

- Be productive and make a positive contribution to the quality of life for themselves and others.

Individuals who wish to help others should begin with some introspection to determine their own motives and progress toward self-reliance. They should become aware of their own attitudes and behaviors as they are likely to impact on their ability to help others with proper intent and effective action.

These few principles are a beginning point. They provide some direction for designing and implementing mentoring efforts and allow a great deal of latitude in how they are implemented through the configurations of mentoring efforts.

Summary

A definition for mentoring has been proposed which defines mentoring as a function with a specific purpose, "To provide a comprehensive effort toward helping the individual develop self-reliance and personal accountability in a defined environment." The proposed definition eliminates many relational and organizational limitations currently imposed on mentoring more out of tradition than necessity. Mentoring of individuals by groups and of groups by individuals are possible configurations which may allow mentoring to better accommodate the limitations and constraints found in educational programs, especially in the induction of beginning teachers into the profession.

A list of 6 principles are presented as a beginning point for future development of a much longer list of mentoring guidelines. These principles are derived from theories of learning, motivation, adult development, and organizations and encourage external validity for mentoring practices and programs.

References

Bandura, A. (1977). Self-efficacy: Toward a unifying theory of behavioral change. *Psychological Review*, **84**, 191-215.

Clawson, J.G. (1980). Mentoring in managerial careers. In C.B. Derr (Ed.)., *Work, family and career*. New York: Praeger Publishing.

Coopersmith, S., and Feldman, R. (1974). Fostering a positive self-concept and high self-esteem in the classroom. In R.H. Coop and K. White (Eds.) *Psychological concepts in the classroom*. New York: Harper & Row.

Glasser, W. (1965). *Reality therapy*. New York: Harper & Row.

Kay, R.S. (1989). *Avoiding hazardous wastes in education: A program for staff development*. Unpublished manuscript.

Levinson, D. (1978). *The seasons of a man's life*. New York: Knopf.

Peck, M.S. (1974). *The road less traveled*. New York: Simon & Schuster.

White,R. (1959). Motivation reconsidered: The concept of competence. *Psychological Review*, **66**(5), 297-333.

Squishy Business

Leslie L. Huling-Austin
Southwest Texas State University

Editors' Introduction: The use of two reactionary statements from ex-perienced teachers guide the author's thrust in interpreting the squishy and tricky business of mentoring. Her interpretation includes three styles of mentoring based on the three styles of change facilitators developed at the R&D Center for Teacher Education.

In recent years, more and more school districts across the county have launched teacher induction programs to assist beginning teachers. Most of these programs include some type of mentor teacher or support teacher component, through which experienced teachers are paired with novice teachers for the purpose of providing them with support and assistance throughout their first year(s) in the classroom. When newly assigned mentor teachers participate in training to help prepare them for their new role, they frequently have one of two reactions which can be summarized by these two comments:

"I think we do that already."

"Tell me exactly what is required of me in this role."

Both of these reactions are quite normal and understandable and serve as useful catalysts for prompting further dialogue about the role and function of the mentor teacher in a beginning teacher program.

"I Think We Do That Already"

A typical starting point for explaining the role of the mentor teacher is to describe the mentor as someone to whom the beginning teacher can go for help or to have questions answered. It is helpful if the mentor's classroom is located near the beginning teacher's classroom so they can have ready access to each other. It is beneficial if both teachers are assigned to teach the same discipline or grade level. When this is the case, the beginning teacher can ask very specific questions of the mentor such as how to introduce certain material, how to pace specific lessons, or how to reinforce difficult concepts. When a specific teacher is assigned to be the mentor, the beginning teacher feels he/she has *permission* to ask for help from this person and the mentor feels that his/her assistance is *sanctioned* rather than likely to be viewed as interference.

Upon hearing this explanation of the mentoring process, new and prospective mentors often conclude that *we do that already* (although perhaps in a more informal sense) and that in their new role as mentors it will largely be *business as usual*. To some degree it is true that they *do that already*. Teachers are certainly to be highly commended for the large amounts of informal mentoring that has taken place in many schools for years, for without it many beginning teachers would have found the transition into teaching more difficult than it has been. Undoubtedly without this informal mentoring even larger numbers of beginning teachers would have experienced severe stress and trauma resulting, for some, in their departure from the profession in their first years of teaching. However, it is this author's contention that when the mentor teacher role is fully actualized, the mentoring process goes far beyond what has taken place in the past in most settings.

A concept that was developed through research conducted at the Research and Development Center for Teacher Education (R&DCTE) and The University of Texas at Austin has been useful in helping to clarify the role of the mentor teacher. Researchers at R&DCTE studied educators in a wide variety of roles who had as a part of their job responsibility the implementation of new educational programs. The purpose of studying these educators, or *change facilitators*, was to learn more about what they did on a day-to-day basis that influenced the implementation process. After extensive study, R&DCTE researchers proposed the concept of *change facilitator style* suggesting that educational leaders approach the change process in quite different ways and that these different styles of facilitating change in fact have a strong influence on the implementation success of change efforts (Hall, Rutherford, Hord, & Huling, 1983). Briefly, the three styles of facilitating change are described below:

> **Responders** — place heavy emphasis on allowing teachers and others the opportunity to take the lead. They believe their primary role is to maintain a smooth running school by focusing on traditional administrative tasks, keeping teachers content and treating students well. They view teachers as strong professionals who are able to carry out their instructional role with little guidance. Responders emphasize the personal side of their relationships with teachers and others. Before they make

decisions they often give everyone an opportunity to have input so as to weigh their feelings or to allow others to make the decision. A related characteristic is the tendency toward making decisions in terms of immediate circumstances rather than in terms of longer range instructional or school goals. This seems to be due in part to their desire to please others and in part to their more limited vision of how their school and staff should change in the future.

Managers — represent a broader range of behaviors. They demonstrate both responsive behaviors in answer to situations or people and they also initiate actions in support of the change effort. The variations in their behavior seem to be linked to their rapport with teachers and central office staff as well as how well they understand and buy into a particular change effort. Managers work without fanfare to provide basic support to facilitate teachers' use of an innovation. They keep teachers informed about decisions and are sensitive to teacher needs. They will defend their teachers from what are perceived as excessive demands. When they learn that the central office wants something to happen in their school they become very involved with their teachers in making it happen. Yet, they do not typically initiate attempts to move beyond the basics of what is imposed.

Initiators — have clear, decisive long-range policies and goals that transcend but include implementation of the current innovation.

They tend to have very strong beliefs about what good schools and teaching should be like and work intensely to attain this vision. Decisions are made in relation to their goals for the school and in terms of what they believe to be best for students, which is based on current knowledge of classroom practice. Initiators have strong expectations for students, teachers and themselves. They convey and monitor these expectations through frequent contacts with teachers and clear explication of how the school is to operate and how teachers are to teach. When they feel it is in the best interest of their school, particularly the students, Initiators will seek changes in district programs or policies or they will reinterpret them to suit the needs of the school. Initiators will be adamant but not unkind. They solicit input from staff, and then make decisions in terms of the goals of the school, even if some are ruffled by their directness and high expectations.

In one extensive study, the Principal-Teacher Interaction Study, it was found that Initiators achieved the highest degree of implementation success, followed by Managers and Responders, respectively. The correlation between change facilitator style and implementation success was found to be .78 which was statistically significant at the .01 level of significance (Huling, Hall, Hord, & Rutherford, 1983).

Mentor teachers are certainly change facilitators in that their role is to help facilitate the teacher induction process and specifically, to help beginning teachers enter the teaching profession. Two observations can be made from the experiences that have occurred in mentoring programs: (1) different mentors conceptualize their role differently, and (2) their conceptualization of the role greatly influences what they do on a day-to-day basis in their interactions with their beginning teacher(s). The similarities between this phenomena and that of change facilitating style has led to the proposed *Styles of Mentoring* suggested in Figure 1. Furthermore, while there has not been research conducted to explore this area, there very likely is a strong relationship between mentoring style and the degree of professional growth experienced by the mentor's protege.

As Figure 1 suggests, each of the three styles carries with it different requirements, results in different outcomes, and has different limitations. Unlike the change facilitating styles, these styles of mentoring have not yet been thoroughly investigated to identify detailed behavioral indicators of each style. Briefly, the three styles of mentoring, as they are currently conceptualized, are described below:

> **Responders** — encourage the beginning teacher to ask for help and provide the requested assistance in the area of concern.

> **Colleagues** — frequently initiate informal visits with the beginning teacher and when the beginning teacher expresses a concern or problem, Colleagues provide assistance related to the area of concern.

> **Initiators** — believe it is their responsibility to facilitate the professional growth of the beginning teacher to the greatest degree possible. In

Figure 1

Styles of Mentoring the Beginning Teacher

Style and Description	Requirements	Outcomes	Limitations
Responder: Encourages BT to ask for help and provides assistance when requested in areas of concern.	MT who is willing to help; BT who trusts the MT enough to ask for help	BT gets help with major areas of concern	Many of the day-to-day problems not dealt with constructively
Colleague: Frequently initiates informal visits with BT and when BT expresses a concern or problem, provides assistance related to the area of concern.	Additional time commitment on part of MT	Stronger personal relationship develops between BT and MT; BT gets substantial help with identified areas of concern	Extent of professional growth determined by BT who has limited experience and view of effective teaching
Initiator: Accepts a responsibility to facilitate the professional growth of the BT to greatest degree possible. In addition to providing assistance when requested, regularly makes suggestions to BT to promote growth.	Substantial teaching expertise on part of MT; Strong rapport between MT and BT; MT must have opportunity to observe teaching of BT	BT gets benefit of the expertise of the MT; MT experiences professional growth as well as BT	Extent of professional growth limited only by the potential of BT and the mentoring expertise of MT

MT = Mentor Teacher; BT = Beginning Teacher

Based in part on the concept of Change Facilitator Style (*c.f.*, Hall, G.E., Rutherford, W.L., Hord, S.M., & Huling, L.L., 1984).

addition to providing assistance when requested, Initiators regularly make suggestions to the beginning teacher to promote growth.

Most likely when informal mentoring has occurred in settings where there is no formal induction program, it has been more the responder style of mentoring. Certainly, in some instances, an experienced teacher has befriended a novice teacher and the colleague style of mentoring has resulted. Instances of this type of mentoring, however, have probably been more the result of teachers having compatible personalities that have led them to form a friendship than it has been by design for intended educational outcomes. Due to the norms of the teaching profession and the constraints and demands of the workplace, the initiator style of mentoring rarely has occurred when the mentoring process has been left to occur through informal channels.

While Figure 1 is generally self-explanatory, a few points are worthy of expansion. The first of these points relates to the limitations of the various styles. When a responder style of mentoring is employed and it is left to beginning teachers to initiate requests for assistance, it is likely that beginning teachers will seek help only when a problem is really pressing because they do not want to overly impose on the mentor teachers. The result is that many of the day-to-day problems are not dealt with constructively, and when left to their own devices to solve a problem in the classroom, beginning teachers may or may not derive a solution that is educationally sound.

While the colleague style of mentoring provides increased interaction between the mentor teacher and the beginning teacher, the beginning teacher is still *in the driver's seat* when determining what areas are in need of attention. While a certain degree of this is desirable, the beginning teacher has very limited experience and is likely to have an immature view of what effective teaching entails. The result is likely to be that many *teachable moments* will be lost and many opportunities for growth will be missed.

When a mentor teacher employs an initiator style of mentoring, additional opportunities for professional growth are opened up for both the beginning teacher and mentor. Also, when mentors seriously begin to focus on helping the beginning teacher become the best teacher possible, they report that they reflect more on their own teaching. During this process, mentors experience professional growth of their own and report feeling more personally rewarded in the role of mentor teacher. Furthermore, the extent of professional growth experienced by the beginning teacher assigned to a mentor employing the initiator style is no longer solely dependent on the beginning teacher's current level of expertise or commitment.

In summary, the concept of mentoring styles is not intended to suggest that there is only one right way to approach the task of mentoring. Certainly, within each of the styles, a wide range of behaviors could and do occur. Rather, these mentoring styles help clarify the opportunities teachers have to maximize the effects of mentoring and to delineate how mentoring can be much more than the *business as usual* approach to mentoring that is employed in many school settings.

"Tell Me Exactly What Is Required of Me in This Role"

It is understandable that newly assigned mentor teachers want their role to be clarified and want to know the exact requirements of their new responsibility. In some mentoring programs there are no *concrete* requirements spelled out for mentor teachers, while in others there is a list of formal requirements such as attending certain training sessions, observing the beginning teacher a set number of times, and completing required forms. However, in both types of programs there is an implicit expectation that the mentor will vary his/her role to meet the needs of the specific beginning teacher. Because of this, it is expected that one mentor will likely fulfill the role in ways that vary substantially from how other mentors may operate. Unfortunately, there is no magic formula for mentoring — mentoring is, in fact, "squishy business."

However, there are factors that can be considered by the mentor teacher when trying to shape his/her role. Again, a previously proposed concept has been adapted to help clarify what some of these factors are and how they might be used to help shape or delineate an appropriate role for a specific mentor teacher. Huling-Austin and Murphy (1987) suggest that the teacher induction process is influenced by the personal and professional characteristics of the beginning teacher, the teaching context, and the induction support program. Because these three factors interact, it is not enough to consider each factor in isolation, but rather, all three factors must be considered in combination. The following equation represents this idea:

Induction Success = f(Beginning Teacher x Context x Support Program)

For the mentor teacher, what this equation should suggest is that the type of assistance a specific beginning teacher will need (and thus the way in which the mentor's role should be shaped) will be determined by the personal and professional characteristics of the beginning teacher, the teaching context, and the total teacher induction support program. The mentor teacher may be just one piece of the overall teacher induction program or the mentor teacher may be the only formal support being offered to the beginning teacher.

An example of how this equation might be useful could go something like this: a beginning teacher with no previous experiences in an inner-city school setting will need a different type of mentoring than one who perhaps grew up in this type of setting and/or did student teaching in such a school. Also, if other components of the school's staff development program are providing training and assistance to the beginning teacher in how to deal with an inner-city school setting, then the mentor might play more of a supporting role. If there is no such additional assistance available, it will probably be necessary for the mentor to deal with this issue much more directly.

To summarize this point, it is important for mentor teachers to be familiar with the school district's requirements of their role, but it is also important for them to realize that much of their role, perhaps even the most important part of their role, cannot be defined for them in advance. If the role of mentor teacher is to be fully actualized, it will be necessary for each mentor teacher to develop his/her own role by considering the individual characteristics and needs of the beginning teacher(s) to whom he or she has been assigned, the teaching context, and the overall teacher induction program.

In Conclusion

The purpose of this chapter was to shed some light on the highly complex process of mentoring. Mentoring is, in fact, squishy business. The solution to the mentoring puzzle is not to become more proficient at *nailing jelly to a tree*. The sooner it is recognized and accepted that both the role of the mentor and the mentoring process are highly complex, the sooner greater degrees of meaningful mentoring will take place between experienced and novice teachers in school settings across the country.

References

Hall, G. E., Rutherford, W.L., Hord, S. M., & Huling, L. L. (1984, February). Effects of three principal styles on school improvement. *Educational Leadership*, **41**(5), 22-29.

Huling, L. L., Hall, G. E., Hord, S. M., & Rutherford, W. L. (1983). *A multi-dimensional approach for assessing implementation success.* Paper presented at the annual meeting of the American Educational research Association, Montreal.

Huling-Austin, L. L., & Murphy, S. C. (1987). *Assessing the impact of teacher induction programs: Implications for program development.* Paper presented at the annual meeting of the American Educational Research Association, Washington, D.C.

A New Knowledge Base for an Old Practice

Theresa M. Bey
The University of Georgia

Editors' Introduction: The author recommends a knowledge base to chart the future direction of a content specific paradigm to prepare mentors. The author suggests that mentors be exposed to an array of experiences and information in the areas of mentoring, clinical supervision, coaching, adult development, and interpersonal skills.

Mentoring in education is an old practice of experienced teachers passing on their expertise and wisdom to new colleagues faced with the challenges of merging theory and practice. Today, this ancient practice is rapidly advancing as school districts create a workplace where student teachers, intern teachers, beginning teachers, and experienced teachers as newly hired employees have mentors to help them cope with the dissatisfactions, disappointments, and difficulties associated with the initial phase of teaching. Having an experienced teacher available to oversee the newcomers entry into the profession is a way of encouraging them to become committed to teaching as a long-term career.

Other elements influencing the use of mentor teachers are complicated circumstances in which school districts suffer from high teacher turnover or a shortage of teachers in critical subject areas such as mathematics and science. To address these problems, beginning teachers are being mentored as a way to improve teacher retention and new teacher performance. This effort to retain teachers has become a major factor within the scope of helping novices survive the first few years. New teachers receive support from colleagues who are knowledgeable about tasks mandated by school policies and tasks required for effective teaching and learning to occur in the classroom.

As the practice of mentoring increases, so does the literature and research on the realities of experienced teachers working with less experienced teachers. The current literature focuses on the mentors' stages of development, functions, and relationships with proteges (Brozoska et al., 1987; Gray & Gray, 1985; Kram, 1983; Shulman & Colbert, 1988). It contains various descriptions of mentoring and offers a general source of information for constructing criteria to direct the mentors' performance (Anderson & Shannon, 1986; Galvez-Hjornevik, 1985; Lambert & Lambert, 1985; Merriam, 1983). An emphasis on gathering more information to reveal the emotional adjustments and attitudinal changes that teachers endure in successful and unsuccessful relationships is also highlighted in the literature (Huffman & Leak, 1986; Levinson et al., 1978; Zey, 1984). Overall, there is an emphasis on increasing the use and availability of information, allowing teachers an opportunity to assume more responsibility in working with beginners (Bova & Phillips, 1984; Gehrke, 1988; Kent, 1985).

This chapter will discuss content related to mentoring from the perspective of preparing teachers to serve as mentors. Furthermore, the information featured in this chapter is only a segment of the content from which one may choose to establish a knowledge base to educate mentors. It offers the framework for identifying sources that describe specific fields of content, skills, and abilities considered important to the practice of mentoring. Likewise, the information is designed to be helpful to individuals involved in the planning and delivery of training for mentors, and to suggest a knowledge base for use with local program goals and priorities when one is implementing, or restructuring a mentor training program.

What's the Knowledge Base?

A review of related literature and research appropriate to recommend as a knowledge base for teachers to learn about mentoring includes business, education, and adult development. Each one recognizes different underlying assumptions about the approaches to mentoring in the workplace, as well as the value of having employees share their expertise with other employees (Hunt & Micheal, 1983; Kahnweiler & Johnson, 1980; Schmidt & Wolfe, 1980).

As for education, it is normal to think of teachers as having the human qualities and willingness to share with others. Such willingness is usually displayed by giving freely of their time, suggestions, and materials to newcomers seeking assistance. Often teachers only expect a word of praise or thanks for helping others to grow professionally. Frequently, friendships and lifetime relationships are formed. With this kind of generosity there might seem to be little need for workshops or training sessions to equip teachers with the spirit of kindness. However, there is a great need to provide teachers with a sense of what is involved when establishing a structured mentor—protege relationship as part of a one-on-one collaborative mentorship.

In some schools mentoring is rooted in standardized procedures where teachers are selected either voluntarily or involuntarily to advise new teachers over a designated period of time. Of course, the procedures differ according to each school, but when the mentors' responsibilities are formalized, training is obviously needed. Given this particular need, training should be conducted with the intent to enhance the abilities of teachers to act as role models for others in the profession (Hanes & Mitchell, 1985; Krupp, 1987; Thies-Sprinthall, 1986).

Five fields of content, the process of mentoring, clinical supervision, coaching and modeling, adult development, and interpersonal skills, have been referenced in Figure 1.

These fields cited in the knowledge base are essential attributes and functions conducted within the context of a mentor — protege relationship. They reflect the various dimensions of mentoring, along with the tasks teachers conduct to support the protege. Inconclusively, the content is an integrated representation of topics from guidance and counseling, adult development, instruction, clinical supervision, communications, and career development. Even though the knowledge base suggested for mentor teachers covers a wide spectrum of fields, a few of them are described in the following discussion on clinical supervision, coaching and modeling instructional skills, adult development, and interpersonal skills.

Figure 1

A Knowledge Base for Mentor Teachers: Significant Resources

Fields of Study	Key Components	Selected References
Mentoring Process	Concept and purpose of Mentoring. Role and Responsibility of mentor. Phases of mentoring relationships. Needs of new teachers.	Anderson & Shannon, 1986; Brozoska, et al., 1987; Huffman & Leak, 1986; Galvez-Hjornevik, 1985; Gray & Gray, 1985; Kram, 1983; Krupp, 1987; Merriam, 1983; Shulman & Colbert, 1988; Thies-Sprinthall, 1986; Veenman, 1984; Zey, 1984.
Clinical Supervision	Analysis of instruction. Classroom visitations. Observation techniques. Conferencing skills.	Acheson & Gall, 1987; Beach & Reinhartz, 1989; Glatthorn, 1984; Glickman, 1981 & 1990; Glickman & Bey, 1990; Goldhammer, et al., 1980.
Coaching & Modeling	Effective instructionalstrategies. Demonstration teaching. Reinforcing teaching effectiveness. Modifying instruction. Maintaining professionalism.	Berlinger & Rosenshine, 1987; Gagne, 1989; Good & Brophy, 1987; Joyce & Showers, 1981; Joyce & Weil, 1986; Rosenshine & Stevens, 1986; Schmidt & Wolf, 1980; Showers, 1983 & 1985; Zumwalt, 1986.
Adult Development	Adult learners. Life cycle changes. Stages of teacher development and growth. Self-reliance and motivation. Stress management.	Arends, 1983; Bova & Phillips, 1983; Burden, 1982; Daloz, 1986; Hanes & Mitchell, 1985; Hunt & Michael, 1983; Kahnweiler & Johnson, 1980; Lambert & Lambert, 1985; Levine, 1987; Levinson, 1978, Newman & Newman, 1987; Sprinthall & Thies-Sprinthall, 1983.
Interpersonal Skills	Communication. Problem solving. Decision making. Active listening.	Bramson, 1981; Cooper, 1988; Greenwood & Parkay, 1989, Wallen, 1972.

Clinical Supervision

Mentors may use clinical supervision to work formally or informally with teachers on the improvement of classroom performance. It is a step-by-step approach that renders non-threatening support and leadership to the neophytes who benefit from assistance. In this approach the beginners can discuss their teaching methods, learn to identify problems and conceive of ways to solve them. Thus, clinical supervision is a means for them to receive guidance and advice for rectifying areas where improvement is needed.

According to Acheson and Gall (1987), the clinical supervision approach to mentoring is a cycle with three specific features: conferencing, observation, and feedback. Within any mentoring relationship conferencing is an on-going activity occurring on a regular basis. However, conferencing as related to supervision involves the discussion of teaching before and after a classroom observation. Holding a conference for the teacher to describe the focus and objective of a lesson before observing a class is known as the pre-observation conference. This particular conference outlines the purpose for the observation and includes details about the data gathering technique a mentor teacher will use when visiting the class.

As part of the observation there are several methods of data collection from which mentors may choose. For instance, handwritten descriptions of classroom activities, an audio cassette tape of verbal interaction, or a video camera recorder to document teacher and student behaviors on tape are practical methods for gathering information. The interpretation and analysis of the observational data are important because they have to be reported to the teacher who was observed. Therefore, the conference following the observation is referred to as the post-conference, a time period when the observer and the teacher review observational findings together to determine which aspects of the teacher's classroom performance need strengthening.

When placed into operation, the clinical supervision process involves several steps:

- pre-observation conference,

- classroom observation,

- interpretation and analysis of observation information, and

- post-observation conference.

In fact, these are the steps that Goldhammer, Anderson, and Krajewski (1980) recommend for repeated use of the cycle with teachers who require continual assistance throughout the school year. Since mentors advise new teachers on a continual basis, clinical supervision is most appropriate. Moreover, it enables mentors to learn how to conference with new teachers, observe classroom teaching, use data collection instruments, and interpret data for the post-observation conference.

Coaching and Modeling Instructional Skills

To promote collegial learning among teachers, Joyce and Showers (1981) advocate encouraging teachers to take the initiative to add new instructional skills to their teaching repertoire. Such initiative is considered coaching among peers and motivates teachers to learn and collaborate for professional growth. This interpretation of coaching affirms the mentors' duties to demonstrate, practice, and transfer new teaching skills to the protege. According to the research of Showers (1983, 1985), new skills are mastered successfully when teachers have the opportunity to observe the skill in others and to practice the new skills until they become a natural part of the regular teaching repertoire.

The acquisition and mastery of new skills consume hours of demonstration and practice time, so teachers do need encouragement, reinforcement, and coaching from their colleagues (Showers, 1985). For highly effective experienced teachers, less coaching may be required to modify or refine old practices. This is not likely to be the case with new teachers, who possess a limited repertoire of teaching strategies. Fortunately, it is possible for them to overcome the shortcomings with experience and time to determine which techniques are satisfactory components of their teaching.

Another significant factor in coaching is that teachers develop and enhance their performance through modeling. Because proteges are inclined to replicate behaviors, mentors must model acceptable teaching and nonteaching practices. In exhibiting nonteaching tasks such as discipline or classroom management, the attitude and cooperation of mentors as members of a school's organization are critical. Essentially, mentors have to realize that coaching and modeling go hand-in-hand, especially since newcomers will base opinions and ideas about teaching on the respect and treatment they receive from others. Furthermore, mentors have to be mindful of the time it takes for a beginner to become proficient in making adjustments to instructional strategies and of the fears they may have about modifying their teaching style.

Adult Development

The mentoring phenomenon in education is linked to the maturation of adults with the desire to help others accomplish certain goals. With a major role in assisting others, mentors could neglect to analyze their own development or fail to remember what it was like during the stages of their development as a new teacher. Consequently, they should be aware of the complexities surrounding the transitions individuals encounter at different periods in the life cycle. Glickman (1990) suggests that cognitive, conceptual, ego, moral, and personality development influence the capabilities of teachers. In fact, the effectiveness of experienced teachers alters over time, causing a change in professional behaviors. Since they are exposed to various changes and experiences, mature teachers are likely to be knowledgeable and at ease in helping new teachers during the initial phase of teaching.

According to Kram (1983) mentoring redirects one's energies into creativity and productivity at midlife. Given these positive attributes, along with the nature of adult growth, there appears to be no problem with older teachers as mentors. Having a different perspective, Zey (1984) refers to the problems and misguided motives of many mentors who assume the task of helping others. In some mentoring relationships, experienced teachers may want to advance their own professional status through the renewal or revitalization they experience from other teachers. Whatever the personal goals may be (according to Levinson et al., 1978, p. 98), a true mentor fosters the young adult's development by believing in him, sharing the youthful dream and giving it his blessing, and creating a space in which the young adult can work on a reasonably satisfactory life structure that contains the dream.

Surely, mentors consider proteges as adults who are capable of developing the characteristics necessary to reach the goal of being an effective teacher. For some proteges, in the early stage of their life cycle, having mentors to lead them can be most beneficial. New teachers who are middle aged or making a midlife career change, however, might regard the benefits of mentoring somewhat differently if they possess the self-assurance and competencies to succeed as beginning teachers. They might prefer the mentors' leadership only long enough to feel comfortable with teaching, whereas young adults lacking the confidence could want the mentors' leadership for a longer period of time.

Throughout the stages of teachers' professional development, teachers possess different job skills, attitudes, behaviors, knowledge and concerns at different points in their career. Burden (1982) identifies these stages as the survival stage, the adjustment stage, and the mature stage. The survival stage is the first year when new teachers are concerned with meeting professional requirements and adjusting to the school's environment. Next, the adjustment stage occurs between the second and fourth year of teaching, a period when teachers strive for growth in classroom techniques and demonstrate increasing confidence. Lastly the mature stage, beginning with the fifth teaching year, teachers tend to feel secure. Even though these three stages are linked to years of experience, developmental patterns also change with the life cycle. Likewise, Levine (1987) supports the importance of understanding the developmental cycle of teachers, as a means of improving job satisfaction and morale. Naturally, the responsibilities mentors undertake in the developmental process of new teachers represent a significant aspect of professional growth and satisfaction.

Interpersonal Skills

Interpersonal skills such as active listening, questioning, problem solving, and decision making are clearly the elements mentors depend upon (Bey, 1990). While conferring with proteges they need the ability to be patient and willing to listen to the little annoyances that upset proteges. In addition, there are times of joy when mentors get to hear about the successes that make teachers happy. As mentors become acquainted with the proteges, they determine appropriate times to ask questions, give advice, or withhold their comments to another time. Tackling problems and making decisions present a crucial dimension for mentors to enlighten new teachers with suggestions or recommendations.

Relating to people in a warm, friendly, caring, and sensitive manner is at the crux of sustaining a mentoring relationship. Being an open and trusting individual with a talent for building a bond for others to express themselves freely is necessary. Another essential quality is to know when too much help is overpowering or is causing the proteges to feel burdened by the relationship. The level of communicative exchange between mentors and proteges is basically messages conveying thoughts, feelings and ideas. Cooper (1988) refers to the influence of intended and unintended messages expressed by teachers in the classroom as contributing to miscommunication. Hopefully, these factors of miscommunication are not leading to misunderstandings in mentoring relationships.

In situations where mentors work hard to maintain healthy lines of communication their proteges, unfortunately, may not always receive positive feedback from supervisors and administrators. In fact, the letter in Figure 2 describes what can happen to a new teacher when the mentor is the only individual assuming the major responsibility for helping her handle difficult problems in a constructive manner.

When reading this letter it is evident that Tom Mentor was willing to teach what he knew about teaching to someone else, once he completed the mentor training session. However, the letter does not give any indication as to whether Tom thought his training was adequate given the type of problems and lack of administrative support he encountered in working with Pauline. If given an opportunity to talk directly to Tom about the knowledge base applied in his training, here are a few questions that one might ask.

• What would you include in a knowledge base to increase the consciousness of what a novice mentor should expect?

Figure 2

A Mentor's Letter*

Dear Theresa:

After the two week training session, I started my mentoring activities on the first work day of September. My protege was Pauline. I found her to have an exciting and enthusiastic attitude toward teaching and mentoring. She seemed to be confident and was looking forward to the challenge of teaching.

I showed her how to use the machines, full out the routine forms, and tried to help her with all facets of planning. I found her a very proud person, one who wanted to do it her way. She did very well to begin with, but her state of mind was impacted first by her supervising teacher who gave her the most degrading rating I have seen for a beginning teacher. This shook her very foundation of confidence, and nothing I said seemed to be any reassurance.

Additional problems came from her classes because of their size. Students were continually added until Pauline had over 36 in her most demanding class. I tried to get the administrators to lessen the load by giving her planning during fourth period instead of hall duty and adjusting her planning to my planning period, but none of these suggestions was deemed possible by the administrators due to the immense problems that would be caused by rescheduling.

She became more frustrated and lost confidence as some of her students became greater behavior problems. I tried to assist in this area by talking to her about behavior problems and by giving her suggestions on how to deal with them on a positive note. We also had several conferences on dealing with parents and getting them involved. I exchanged my sixth period class with her for a day so that I could get a better feeling for the types of students that she was dealing with on the academic level. I also wanted to observe the behavior of the students.

I found her students to be very responsive for the most part, but there were three who had a "big chip on their shoulders." It was these three who later affected her attitude more than I guessed.

Next, I had the media specialist to help me tape Pauline's class, but this did not prove to be too successful on the first attempt due to the malfunction of the equipment. Three days later, I got a paraprofessional to cover my class and once again I made an attempt to video tape the class. I used an adjoining room that had windows facing her class. We had some success and she took the film home to view it.

Pauline seemed to be doing all right, but little did I realize the depths of her depression and despair over her predicaments. I discovered from another teacher, who had also been assisting me with her, that Pauline had resigned. Pauline apologized for not telling me, but she said she did not want me talking her out of it.

I then talked to Pauline's department chairperson and found that she had done nothing to help her. The department chairperson's attitude reflected that of the administrators'. The chairperson felt that Pauline was hired to do a job and she should take care of it.

I had also tried to arrange a breakfast with Pauline and her instructional supervisor, but the supervisor would not come. I had hoped that breakfast with the supervisor, the department head, the principal, and me would begin to change Pauline's attitude and make her feel that she had a support group. It is a shame that this did not come to pass.

This has been a disappointing but enlightening experience. I am of the opinion that the administrators have to take a more conscientious role in helping the new teacher. In fact, nothing a mentor does is as significant as the instructional supervisor's role. All of the supervisors need to re-examine their position and attitude toward working with young people. I am of the opinion that a superfluous air of importance makes the attitude of supervisors seem callous, and as a result, they sometimes can not relate to the persons they supervise.

In closing, I sometimes wonder if we try to get rid of new teachers before they've learned the ropes? How many of us might have become a Pauline had we gone through what she did? Remember that Pauline had a good outlook that went sour.

Your friend,

Tom Mentor

---

*Although this represents an actual letter received by the author, the names have been changed.

- Did the level of knowledge presented in the training prepare you to take on all the responsibilities related to a new teacher?

- What type of problem-solving skills made it possible to handle the frustrations you experienced as a mentor?

Responses to these questions would provide some insight regarding the usefulness of the content and knowledge presented in Tom's training session.

Moreover, the elements of making decisions and solving problems are qualities which mentors must rely on when fulfilling the duties to advise newcomers. Besides, as experienced teachers strive to refine their interpersonal skills, situations and conflicts in which no advanced preparation can help them avoid or resolve shall continue to occur.

Summary

In conclusion, several fields of study are suggested in this chapter as a knowledge base for mentor teachers. They include the mentoring process, clinical supervision, coaching and modeling instructional skills, adult development, and interpersonal skills. On the chart listing significant resources, each field contains a variety of resources which can be tailored to accommodate the needs of both novice and experienced mentor teachers. To be more specific, information on the mentoring process presents a view of the mentor's role, responsibilities, and relationship with the protege. The clinical supervision field places an emphasis on supervisory techniques and classroom observation. As a means of striving for continual teacher effectiveness and improvement, coaching and modeling instructional skills are highlighted. Then, the purpose of understanding the adult learner and stages of professional growth, adult development is also featured. Lastly, the field of interpersonal skills refers to communicative aspects of the mentor's performance.

Collectively, these fields of study represent a broad range of content. So, when a program planner decides on a knowledge base for mentor teachers to become competent in their role, prerequisites such as years of teaching experience, teaching proficiency, and previous experiences in assisting other teachers have to be considered. Another consideration is the identification of mentors who need introductory content to gain an awareness of their role as opposed to those needing content to enhance their mentoring skills. In determining the mentors' level of knowledge, the program goals, purpose for mentoring, and training of mentors are also important considerations.

A well planned knowledged base is a springboard for advancing the development of mentor teachers, but it also requires practical experiences as a supplement. Content alone is not enough, because some mentoring skills and abilities are only learned effectively through practice. For example, interpersonal skills, listening skills, and people skills are areas that are enriched through the real experience of being a mentor. Therefore, the proper application of a new knowledge base is deemed suitable to the old and valued practice of mentoring the new teacher.

References

Acheson, K. A., & Gall, M. D. (1987). *Techniques in the clinical supervision of teachers* (2nd ed.). New York: Longman.

Anderson, E. M., & Shannon, S. L. (1986). Toward a conceptualization of mentoring. *Journal of Teacher Education*, **39**(1), 38-42.

Arends, R. I. (1983). Beginners teachers as learners. *Journal of Educational Research*, **76**, 235-242.

Beach, D. M., & Reinhartz, J. (1989). *Supervision: Focus on instruction*. New York: Harper and Row.

Berliner, D. C., & Rosenshine, B. V. (Eds.). (1987). *Talks to teachers*. New York: Random House.

Bey, T. M. (1990). *Preparing mentor teachers*. Unpublished manuscript. Athens, The University of Georgia.

Bey, T. M. (1989). *Teacher education and mentoring program: Program design and research results*. Unpublished manuscript. Athens, The University of Georgia.

Bova, B. M., & Phillips, R. R. (1984). Mentoring as a learning experience for adults. *Journal of Teacher Education*, **35**(3), 16-20.

Bramson, R. M. (1981). *Coping with difficult people*. New York: Random House.

Brozoska, T., Jones, J., Mahaffy, J., Miller, J. K., & Mychals, J. (1987). *Mentor Teacher Handbook*. Portland, OR: Northwest Regional Laboratory.

Burden, P. R. (1982, February). *Developmental supervision: Reducing teacher stress at different career stages*. Paper presented at the annual conference of the Association for Teacher Educators, Phoenix, AZ (ERIC Document Reproduction Service No. ED 218 267)

Cooper, P. J. (1988). *Speech communication for the classroom teacher* (3rd ed.). Scottdale, AZ: Gorsuch Scarisbrick, Publishers.

Daloz, L. A. (1986). *Effective teaching and mentoring*. San Francisco, CA: Jossey-Bass Publishers.

Gagne, R. M. (1989). *The conditions of learning and theory of instruction*, (5th ed.). New York: Holt, Rinehart and Winston.

Galvez-Hjornevik, C. (1985). *Teacher mentors: A review of the literature*. Austin: University of Texas, Research and Development Center for Teacher Education. (ERIC Document Reproduction Service No. ED 263 105).

Gehrke, N.J. (1988). On preserving the essence of mentoring as one form of teacher leadership. *Journal of Teacher Education*, **39**(1), 43-45.

Glatthorn, A. A. (1984). *Differentiated supervision*. Alexandria, VA: Association for Supervision and Curriculum Development. (ERIC Document Reproduction Service No. ED 245 401)

Glickman, C.D. (1990). *Supervision of instruction: A developmental approach* (2nd ed.). Boston: Allyn and Bacon.

Glickman, C. D. (1981). *Developmental supervision: Alternative practices for helping teachers improve instruction.* Alexandria, VA: Association for Supervision and Curriculum Development.

Glickman, C. D., & Bey, T. M. (1990). Supervision. In W. R. Houston (Ed.)*Handbook of Research on Teacher Education.* New York: Macmillan.

Goldhammer, R., Anderson, R. H., & Krajewski, R. J. (1980). *Clinical supervision: Special methods for the supervision of teachers* (2nd ed.). New York: Hold, Rinehart and Winston.

Good, T. L., & Brophy, J. E. (1987). *Looking in classrooms* (4th ed.). New York: Harper & Row.

Gray, W. A., & Gray, M. M. (1985). Synthesis of research on mentoring beginning teachers. *Educational Leadership,* **43**(3), 37-43.

Greenwood, G. E. & Parkay, F. W. (1989). *Case studies for teachers decision making.* New York: Random House.

Hanes, R. C., & Mitchell, K. F. (1985). Teacher career development in Charlotte-Mecklenburg. *Educational Leadership,* **43**(3), 11-13.

Huffman, G., & Leak, S. (1986). Beginning teacher's perceptions of mentors. *Journal of Teacher Education,* **37**(1), 22-25.

Hunt, D. M., & Michael, C. (1983). Mentorship: A career training and development tool. *Academy of Management Review*, **8**(3), 475-485.

Joyce, B. R., & Showers, B. (1981). Transfer of training: The contribution of coaching. *Journal of Education*, **163**(2), 163-172.

Joyce, B., & Weil, M. (1986). *Models of teaching* (2nd ed.). Englewood Cliffs, NJ: Prentice-Hall.

Kahnweiler, J., & Johnson, P. (1980). A mid-life development profile of the returning female student. *Journal of College Student Personnel*, **21**, 414-419.

Kent, K. K (1985). A successful program of teachers assisting teachers. *Educational Leadership*, **43**(3), 30-33.

Kram, K. E. (1983). Phases of the mentor relationship. *Academy of Management Journal*, **26**(4), 608-625.

Krupp, J. A. (1987). Mentoring: A means by which teachers become staff developers. *Journal of Staff Development*, **8**(1), 12-15.

Lambert, L., & Lambert, D. (1985). Mentor teachers as change facilitators. *Thrust for Educational Leadership*, **14**(6), 28-32.

Levine, S. L. (1987). Understanding life cycle issues: A resource for school leaders. *Journal of Education*, 169(1), 7-19.

Levinson, D. J., Darrow, C., Klein, E., Levinson, M., &

McKee, B. (1978). *The season's of a man's life*. New York: Alfred A. Knopf.

Merriam, S. (1983). Mentors and proteges. A critical review of the literature. *Adult Education Quarterly*, **33**(3), 161-173.

Newman, B. M., & Newman, P. R. (1987). *Development through life: A psychosocial approach* (4th ed.). Chicago: Dorsey Press.

Rosenshine, B., & Stevens, R. (1986). Teaching functions. In M. Wittrock (Ed.), *Third handbook of research on teaching*. New York: Macmillan.

Schmidt, J. A., & Wolf, J. S. (1980). The mentor partnership: Discovery of professionalism. *National Association of student Personnel Administrations Journal*, **17**, 45-51.

Showers, B. (1985). Teachers coaching teachers. *Educational Leadership*, **42**(7), 43-48.

Showers, B. (1983). *Transfer of training: The contribution of coaching*. Eugene, OR: Center Educational Policy and Management, University of Oregon. ED

Shulman, J. H., & Colbert, J. A. (Eds.), (1988). *Mentor teacher casebook*. San Francisco: Far West Laboratory for Educational Research and Development.

Sprinthall, N., & Thies-Sprinthall, L. (1983) The teacher as an adult learner: A cognitive-developmental view. In G. Griffin (Ed.). *Staff Development*.

Chicago: University of Chicago Press.

Thies-Sprinthall, L. (1986). A collaborative approach for mentoring training: A working model. *Journal of Teacher Education*, **37**(6), 13-20.

Veenman, S. (1984). Perceived problems of beginning teachers. *Review of Educational Research*, **54**(2), 143-178.

Wallen, J. L. (1972). Effective interpersonal communications. In R. Pino, R. Emory, and C. Jung. *Interpersonal communications*. Portland, OR: Northwest Regional Educational Laboratory.

Zey, M. G. (1984). *The mentor connection.* Homewood, IL: Dow Jones-Irwin.

Zumwalt, K. K. (Ed.)., (1986). *ASCD yearbook: Improving teaching*. Alexandria, VA: Association for Supervision and Curriculum.

A Recapitulation

C. Thomas Holmes
The University of Georgia

Although all personnel administration text books point out the need for effective induction programs for new employees, the typical program in a school system has generally consisted of a short informational program conducted during preplanning week. Until new teachers become fully adjusted to teaching and its demands, the school and community environments, and the faculty with its expectations, they cannot be expected to perform at their highest level. Many capable individuals have given up teaching as a result of a particularly unpleasant or frustrating first year that may have been avoided with a comprehensive induction program.

Sandra Odell introduced us to a concept of mentoring as an effective component of the induction program. She allowed that in the context of schools, a mentor is most likely to limit the focus to the professional growth of a new teacher. She additionally argued that a mentor must be an excellent classroom teacher, must possess wisdom and skills in listening and questioning, and be facile at conflict resolution. The mentoring relationship requires fostering that it may develop into a "significant" relationship.

Richard Kay, in his chapter, contended that much of the literature on mentoring was focused on describing what existing mentoring programs were like. He, on the other hand, defined mentoring as "providing a comprehensive effort toward helping the individual develop self-reliance and personal accountability in a defined environment." Based on his definition, he provided us with a look at what mentoring "should be."

Leslie Huling-Austin then provided a model of mentoring based on three styles: Responder, Colleague, and Instructor. The appropriate style depends on the specific needs of the new teacher, the characteristics of the mentor, and the characteristics of the overall induction program.

Thersa Bey then suggested an outline of the specific knowledge an individual must possess to be an effective mentor. This knowledge which comes from 5 different fields of study (mentoring process, clinical supervision, coaching and modeling, adult development, and interpersonal skill) should form the basis of any in-service program designed to develop mentors.

This monograph provided pictures of what mentoring programs, as parts of induction programs, might look like and explained how they might work.

Notes on Contributors

Theresa M. Bey is associate professor of instructional supervision in the Department of Curriculum and Supervision in the College of Education at The University of Georgia. She has consulted with teachers and administrators across the United States. Her research interests include the training of mentors, teacher effectiveness, and student underachievement. She is active in the Association of Teacher Educators and serves as chair of the Commission on the Role and Preparation of Mentor Teachers.

Carl D. Glickman is director of the Program for School Improvement and a Professor in the Department of Curriculum and Supervision at The University of Georgia. He has been a school teacher, teaching principal, supervisory principal of alternative schools, and an education analyst and has been a consultant and speaker to education associations throughout the United States, Canada, and Western Europe. He has written numerous articles and is the co-author of the books: *Leadership Guide to Elementary School Improvement* and *Solving Discipline Problems* both published by Allyn and Bacon and author of *Developmental Supervision: Alternative Practices for Helping Teachers Improve Instruction* published by the ASCD and *Supervision of Instruction: A Developmental Approach* published by Allyn and Bacon.

C. Thomas Holmes is Associate Professor of Educational Administration in the College of Education at The University of Georgia. His expertise is in personnel administration which includes employee induction. In addition he has written extensively in the area of research and policies of grade-level retention.

Leslie L. Huling-Austin is director of the LBJ Institute for the Improvement of Teaching and Learning and associate professor of secondary education in the School of Education, Southwest Texas State University, San Marcos. She was previously a program director at the Research and Development Center for Teacher Education at the University of Texas. There she was also principal investigator of the Model Teacher Induction project and coordinator of the Teacher Induction Network. Further, she managed the study, Teacher Induction in Diverse Settings, involving 26 institutions across the nation. Huling-Austin has written extensively in the field of teacher induction programs and internships for the *Handbook of Research on Teacher Education*, to be released by ATE and MacMillan in 1990.

Richard S. Kay is associate professor of educational psychology at Brigham Young University-Utah. He completed his graduate work in 1972 earning a Ph.D. in educational psychology with a minor in child and adolescent development from Purdue University. He developed a strong professional interest in the area of self-concept development in children and adolescents. Kay developed a self-concept development model that has been expanded to become a comprehensive model of education and parenting. Further extension of these same ideas is found in *A Responsibility Model for Mentoring* discussed briefly in his chapter. Kay has been actively involved in mentoring research, writing , and development since 1980.

Sandra J. Odell is director of the Elementary Graduate Intern and Teacher Induction Program and associate professor in the College of Eduction, University of New Mexico, Albuquerque. The program she directs was the 1985 recipient of the American Association of Colleges for Teacher Education's Distinguished Achievement Award. Odell's current research focuses on the needs and the concerns of new teachers in induction contexts, on the impact of induction programs on new teachers, and on retention.

Name Index